A Feast of Prayers

A Feast of Prayers

Liturgy to Holy Mystery

by
Beverly Lanzetta

BLUE SAPPHIRE BOOKS

A Feast of Prayers: Liturgy to Holy Mystery
Copyright © 2021 by Beverly Lanzetta
All rights reserved.

No part of this book may be reproduced in any manner whatsoever without written permission of the publisher except for brief quotations embodied in critical articles or reviews. For information, write: marketing@bluesapphirebooks.com

Prayers on pages 72-78, written by Beverly Lanzetta, first appeared in *40-Day Journey with Joan Chittister* edited by Beverly Lanzetta copyright © 2007 Augsburg Fortress. Used and adapted by permission.

Blue Sapphire Books website http://bluesapphirebooks.com

Cover and interior design: Nelson Kane
Cover art adapted from *Pace e Bene* by Beverly Lanzetta

PUBLISHER'S CATALOGING-IN-PUBLICATION DATA
(Prepared by The Donohue Group, Inc.)

Names: Lanzetta, Beverly, author.
Title: A feast of prayers : liturgy to holy mystery / by Beverly Lanzetta.
Description: [Phoenix, Arizona] : Blue Sapphire Books, [2021]
Identifiers: ISBN 9780984061679 (paperback) | ISBN 9780984061686 (ebook)
Subjects: LCSH: Devotional calendars--Prayers and devotions. | Prayers. | Devotional exercises. | LCGFT: Prayers.
Classification: LCC BV4811 .L36 2021 (print) | LCC BV4811 (ebook) | DDC 242/.2--dc23ared by The Donohue Group, Inc.)

Printed in the United States of America

Contents

Preface   *i*

The Liturgy to Holy Mystery:

    The Vigils   *1*

    Prayers for Days of the Week   *7*

Prayers for Days of Rest and other Occasions   *51*

Forty Days of Prayers   *71*

Prayer of the Universal Monk   *79*

Preface

This little book is a call to daily prayer. It expresses the song of the soul, an inner depth of feeling spontaneously overflowing in words of praise, petition, thanksgiving, and lament. When we speak these words, they become an offering of our heart's devotion. Yet, these prayers are not ours alone, for prayers claim their own liturgical relevance. Recited during designated times of the day, they have their work to do in our souls and in our world.

The impulse to pray is universal. From the moment of birth, until death stills our breath, each human heart, each soul, recites a ceaseless prayer, the very existence of our spirit in physical form an invocation toward the divine. Prayer is the language of the spirit. It is our first language.

Present in every religion and culture, prayer speaks to what we truly feel. It gives permission to be passionate, surrendered—to prostrate on the Earth and ask for guidance, to kneel before an altar or a majestic mountain and allow grace to work in the soul, to cry out in anguish, and to plead for the ability to remember the gift.

I believe that our prayers are heard, the cosmos listens to our vibrations, and God's ears are receptive to our words. Walking in the hills, we hear quail whispering peace prayers. We watch nature praying: the falcon making circles in the air, a heron strolling through a vineyard, and the song of the Blue Oak's leaves rustling in the wind.

Prayer is everywhere. And we bring it everywhere with us. It is an energy that flows into and out of our souls with each breath, curling and somersaulting in spirals, until letters settle in our mind, and then, caught up in the torrential waters of spirit soon become a rain of words. We cling to these lofty sounds, riding the wave of awe, straight back into the Divine Heart.

So, lie down on the Earth, feel the soil pulsing, the ants humming, the gophers digging. Are these not prayers? So, too, are the kettle on the stove, and the casserole in the oven, the dishes being washed, and the dog being fed.

Give us all your prayers, O Holy Life!! We want to absorb them into our souls, to unite with creation's extreme audacity of devotion. Even when we do not know we are praying the universe is praying in us.

Suggestions for praying with this book:

The Liturgy to Holy Mystery includes five prayers per day in a weekly cycle. The liturgy can be used in our daily prayers and also with people gathered in retreat. When the liturgy is spoken, alone or in community, the prayers establish a spirit of peace, enclosing participants in a sacred ritual. Following a prayer cycle during designated times of the day, opens us to an embodied prayer-speaking that binds our hearts to the Divine Presence in our midst.

The Liturgy to Holy Mystery

The Vigils

Vigil: a period of being awake during the time we usually sleep, to keep watch and pray.

Morning Vigil: pray in early hours before dawn, or any time before the active day begins.

Night Vigil: pray after the day ends, when it is dark, usually in the hours after midnight when the world is quiet. Or pray before going to sleep.

Suggestions for the Vigils

Pray the vigils each morning and each night as described above. Pray the vigils for special occasions, such as a vigil for peace, a vigil for a loved one, a vigil for healing, a vigil for the deceased. Pray anytime your spirit is called.

Prayers for Days of the Week

The morning, noon, and evening prayers are designed to be used in a weekly rotation over the months. The reader, of course, can say these prayers in whatever manner—spontaneously, in a regular pattern, on special occasions, and so forth.

Suggestions for a Daily Prayer Schedule

Pray the Morning Vigil

Pray Morning, Noon, and Evening Prayers

Pray the Night Vigil

Prayers for Days of Rest and Other Occasions: This collection includes gathering prayers, closing prayers, ritual prayers, prayers to Holy Sophia, and benedictions for personal and communal devotions, or to expand the daily liturgy.

Forty Days of Prayer: Small prayers to bring the sacred into our lives each day. Helpful when used as a series of prayers for a period of self-reflection alone or in community, during holy days and times of deepening devotion.

Prayer of the Universal Monk: An invocation to the monk within all of us, and the yearning to live in the light of the Holy.

※

It is my hope that *A Feast of Prayers: Liturgy to Holy Mystery* brings solace and joy to your daily devotions, calling each of us to the universal song of love imprinted in our depth.

Beverly Lanzetta
Living in the Desert
2021

LITURGY *to* HOLY MYSTERY

The Vigils

MORNING VIGIL

Canticle of Dawn

> Miracle of sun
> Mystery of cell
> Glorious body
> Blessed are you!
>
> Mother of matter
> Radiant of flesh
> Within you, Spirit
> Dwells on Earth!
>
> House of wisdom
> Resilient of heart
> Teach me compassion
> To love all!
>
> Earth is my body
> Spirit my soul
> Mystery unending
> Joy of great light!

Holy Comes the Dawn!
Grant me this day
    the strength of your path
    the courage of truth
    the practice of nonharm
    the alleviation of suffering
    the passion to find you
    in all things.

Amen.

NIGHT VIGIL

Canticle of Silence

> O Radiant Silence!
>> Into your darkening shadow and
>>> starry sky
>> I commit my soul
>
>> Take me to Your Temple
>> Where spirits rest and heaven is still
>> There, to enter your secret enclosure
>> The measure of my monk's heart.
>
> O Hidden Silence!
>> I entrust my soul to divine benevolence
>> I offer my soul to the healing of the
>>> planet
>> I abandon my soul to wordless bliss
>> Annihilated by your formless mercy.

O Dark Silence!
    Teach me to be a vessel of simplicity
    Help me to receive your generosity
    May I be overcome with tender kisses.

    Teach me to be a messenger of peace
    Help me to receive your wisdom
    May I be overcome with great truth.

    Teach me to be a devotee of love
    Help me to receive your mercy
    May I be overcome with endless compassion.

I long for pure Intimacy!
OM.

LITURGY *to* HOLY MYSTERY

Prayers *for*
Days *of the* Week

MORNING PRAYER ONE

Canticle of Praise (a movement prayer)

Holy Earth, Holy Cosmos,
I bow before you
With my whole being.

Holy Creatures, Holy Nature,
I kneel upon the earth
In honor and thanksgiving
Of your blessed bounty.

Holy Waters, Holy Mountains,
I lay my body on your temple
In gratefulness for nurturing
My tender soul.

Holy Passion, Holy Longing,
I rise up before you
A devotee of truth,
Following wherever you lead me.

Holy Silence, Holy Solitude,
I place my hands over my heart
Breathing in serenity,
Breathing out your peace.

Holy Sorrow, Holy Suffering,
I close my hands in prayer
May I bear every wound
With compassion and nonharm.

Holy Humility, Holy Emptiness,
I bow my head before you
I have become nothing,
For your All to shine in my soul.

Holy Freedom, Holy Rejoicing,
I open my heart to the world
Offering myself to this day,
In joyfulness and gratitude.

Amen.

NOON PRAYER ONE

Canticle of Desire

In the stillness of noon prayer,
    I long for you
Inflame my soul with love's desire
I am your disciple.

In the silence of meditation,
    I long for you
Take my life for your own
I am your disciple.

In the busyness of the day,
    I long for you
Harness my heart for your work
I am your disciple.

In the warmth of family and friends,
    I long for you
Use my joy for the world's awakening
I am your disciple.

You called and I said: "Take me!"
Now, I await your touch
Do not abandon me Great Silence
I am your disciple.

Amen.

EVENING PRAYER ONE

Canticle of Healing

Radiant Spirit, please hear my prayers:

For the dying and the ill,
send the light of solace.

For the violated and rejected,
send the angels of healing.

For the wounded and killed in war,
send the serenity of peace.

For the poor and homeless,
send the heart of compassion.

For the betrayed and abandoned,
send the guardians of love.

For the Earth and all our relations,
Let there be reconciliation.

For the mass of humanity
    without food,
    without parents,
    in poverty,
    alone and bereft
    May my heart break open,
    May I bear suffering in your name.

Make of my soul a home for the homeless
    and a refuge for the poor.
Grant me the strength to be a
    person of healing.

Amen.

MORNING PRAYER TWO

Canticle of Adoration

    O Glorious One, form my heart into a
        bouquet of love:
    May each breath be in praise of you
    May each word announce your holy presence
    May each action honor your hidden glory

    I am a devotee of emptiness
    seeking neither my own name nor will
    but only your desire

    I am a devotee of humility
    offering myself over to your wisdom
    free of self-interest

    I am a devotee of patience
    listening for your voice
    in every word and sigh

    I am a devotee of peace
    with a heart free from resentment
    wide open to love

I am a devotee of compassion
nurturing every pain and sorrow
as my own

I am a devotee of gratitude
giving myself in service of love
in daily wonder of life's gift

I am a devotee of gentleness
into the harsh world I vow to bring
tenderness and loving-kindness

I am a devotee of prayer
whose heart is attuned to your rhythm,
my every breath whispering your name

May this day be filled with flowers and
    fragrances
in celebration of your mystery.

Shalom!

NOON PRAYER TWO

Canticle of Love

    As I gaze upon the noonday sun,
    Tears of joy fall from my eyes
    For the gift of you, Eternal Mother,
    My intimate friend.

    With gentleness you gave of yourself
        the sun to warm my soul
        rain to moisten my tears
        wild desert, mountain redwoods
        and oceans, wide and deep.

    Dearest Mother,
        How I love you!

    Faithfully in
        pain   Gently with
        sorrow   hope
        despair   passion
        sickness   abandon
        confusion   joy
        and darkness   ecstasy
                               and my All

Spiritually through
    your prophets   Creatively in
    saints   animals
    scriptures   plants
    religions   insects
    sacraments   minerals
    rituals   mountains
    and holy places   waters
                                and in matter itself

I love you
    because I love you
        without demand or desire
I love you for you alone
    I want nothing but you
I love you unbounded
    with my heart open in adoration
I love you in emptiness
    when I am most nothing
I love you in freedom
    my soul a feast of prayers.

Amen.

EVENING PRAYER TWO

Canticle of Union

>Holy Mystery, prepare me for your
>>Night Vow:
>
>In the beginning,
>as it is now and ever shall be,
>my life is yours.
>
>I rest upon your verdant meadow,
>sweet breezes adorn my soul
>Your circle of saints surrounds me
>placing flowered garlands upon my head.
>
>Soothed by your Luminous Darkness,
>A chorus of prayers liberates my sins
>I am anointed with sweet oils

O Holy One, may I be worthy of your gift.

I surrender myself to you, Beloved,
our union consecrated by fire
Now your life lives in me
my nothingness is Your All.

Amen.

MORNING PRAYER THREE

Canticle of Creation

    O Radiant Earth and Spirits of Nature!
        I call upon you!
    Open my heart to love
    in every action and in all of creation.

    Mother Earth,
    gestating in the womb of your red clay
    consecrated by the family of matter
    I am your offspring!

    Sea water flows through my cells
    clouds cast shadows over my heart,
    blood of bison in my veins,
    raven wind speaks to me
    Beauty fells my soul!

    Thus comes morning, whispering
    Holy, Holy, Holy
    then a chorus of voices,
    Mother wakes up from slumber,
    healing occurs nightly in the temple
        of dreams.

Come! Sky, Star, Planet
I am made of dust.
Where heaven kisses earth,
I am vastness and silence
Where souls are restored by
    drops of night,
I, too, am family.

Amen.

NOON PRAYER THREE

Canticle of Sorrow

    Take my life and use it for your work,
    May my soul be a home for the homeless
    My heart a sanctuary of mercy
    My actions the measure of devotion

    Please grant us everlasting peace.

    I know suffering and weep
    I know greed and weep
    I know violence and weep
    I know war and weep
    I know desecration and weep

    Expand my heart to hold the suffering
        of the world
    May my life work to heal injustice and oppression
    May my love bring about renewal and hope
    Quench my thirst for truth in thought, word,
        and deed.

How my soul is saddened by
    Your Suffering!
Help me to be Your Heart in this world!

Please grant us everlasting peace.

Amen.

EVENING PRAYER THREE

Canticle of Solitude

When all is still and night descends
    upon the soul
the heart yearns for love's serene
    abandonment.
In the solitary night, when no mortal
    eye beholds,
I lay down my fear and await your
    holy embrace.

My defenses are abandoned
Pride, despair, and shame seared
    by your flame.
Splendid, unfettered self: not this or that!
I am home with no name.

Drawn into God's abode of radiant, silken light
My soul is adorned with blessed simplicity.
Nothing else matters, nothing else holds,
All is yours, none other abides.

I am betrothed to Silence
Taking my vow into the reverie of night.
For I am a devotee of solitude
The monk who lives for you alone.

Amen.

MORNING PRAYER FOUR

Canticle of Light

>Most Holy Presence of Light:
>
>I am grateful for the bounty of the Earth
>>the beauty of the day's awakening
>>the joy of being alive
>
>O Morning of Abundance
>O Morning of Possibility
>O Morning of Innocence
>
>In the hidden chambers of my heart,
>I bow before your radiance,
>>splendid and unearned
>>praying to be worthy of
>>heavenly generosity
>
>O Light Divine
>O Light brighter than the sun
>O Light of Spirit unfurling

May I grow ever closer to the awakening
of your Holy Presence.

Amen.

NOON PRAYER FOUR

Canticle of Humility

>Great Spirit:
>
>Of all the gifts you have given us
>   Humility, most powerful
>   and mysterious
>   calls me to the modesty that
>your goodness desires.
>
>May I take small steps today
>May I greet the ascending light
>   unencumbered, receptive
>
>May I learn to bow and speak words
>   of gratitude
>May I learn to forgive and let myself
>   be forgiven

May I give up pretense, ambition,
    and self-promotion
for the Great Wonder
    that bends my soul in awe!

Amen.

EVENING PRAYER FOUR

Canticle of Dreams

> As shadows soothe the light and a curtain of
> darkness falls before my eyes,
> may I celebrate and dance before
> your Great Mystery
>
> As my soul prepares for its night journey and
> the star of destiny frees my daily cares,
> may I enter your Temple of Solitude
> to bathe in eternal energies.
>
> How grateful am I for my life
> the love shared,
> the simplicity of devotion!

How blessed am I to join
    your Eternal Presence
in my dreams!

Amen.

MORNING PRAYER FIVE

Canticle of Peace

> When day cedes to night
> and creatures large and small
> bow their heads in sweet surrender
> My soul rejoices in
> Your serene embrace.
>
> When spirit fills with starlight
> and dreams of quiet wonder
> wrap me in angelic radiance
> My soul delights in
> Your eternal tranquility.
>
> When I awake in the silken dawn
> awash with the gentle touch of
> Your sweet love
> May I, Holy One, greet the rising sun
> with Blessed Simplicity

Now, I step into the bustle,
now I pray and work
now I struggle and rejoice,
In all,
You are my Peace.

Amen.

NOON PRAYER FIVE

Canticle of the Holy

O Holy One
> May your strength guide me today,
> May I overflow with enthusiasm
> my creative spirit revealed,
> your light shining through me
> into the hearts of all who seek.

O Holy One
> May I discover a new innocence,
> May I celebrate the gift of life
> the pain I carry released,
> your joyful embrace sheltering me
> as I breathe in your love.

O Holy One
> May your light be my light,
> your heart my heart,
> your love my love,
> your grace my grace,
> until I am none other than united with you,
> in thought, word, and deed.

O Holy One
>How I yearn to rest in the joyful abundance of You.

Amen.

EVENING PRAYER FIVE

Canticle of Forgivenes

Dusk of Night, sublime!

Grant me the strength to follow your Way,
the courage to live truth,
the commitment to nonharm,
the faith to enter the nothingness,
the wisdom to endure suffering,
and the passion of your jubilation.

Holy of Holies
Gentle is your Way
Glorious your Name!

Anoint me with love

Your truth be mine
Your will be mine
Your peace be mine
On Earth

Lead me to your heart
Protect me from going astray
Teach me to be humble

Anoint me with compassion

My sins wound you
Forgive me
My sins wound others
Forgive me
My sins wound creation
Forgive me

Amen.

MORNING PRAYER SIX

Canticle of Compassion

>May I be Mindful
>
>May my day begin in mindfulness,
>   aware of the divine flame within.
>May I share love with all of creation,
>   in gratitude and compassion.
>
>May I open my heart to all who suffer today,
>   those I meet and whom I may never meet.
>May I understand how suffering wounds your
>   tender heart, piercing my humanity with grief.
>
>May my being, broken open by the glory
>   and suffering of the world be transformed
>   into a wish-fulfilling jewel.

May my heart this day be beautiful,
>   illumined by fire, enlightened by wisdom
>   and softened by compassion.

May joy burst forth from my presence,
>   like a bouquet of flowers in full bloom!

Amen.

NOON PRAYER SIX

Canticle of Mother

O Great Mother!
A child of your inexhaustible sweetness
May I be worthy of your pure love.

I offer myself as a monk of silence
I offer myself as a monk of gentleness
I offer myself as a monk of happiness
I offer myself as a monk of mercy
I offer myself as a monk of compassion
I offer myself as a monk of peace

May my daily actions be a tribute to you
May my entire being long for justice
May Holy Wisdom flourish within me.

I live for you and in you
    Please do not reject me
I give myself to the divine light
    Please illuminate my soul
I want to be a saint for you
    Please accept me
I want to be holy like you
    Please anoint me

I do not know where you send me, but my fidelity
    is yours
I do not know what you ask of me, but my will
    is yours
I do not know what you desire of me, but my heart
    is yours

What do you ask of me?
    I am yours.

Amen.

EVENING PRAYER SIX

Canticle of Mercy

May I find in my soul the inner cloister
>where Divine Mystery arrives in the night
without sound.

May I be drawn into the pageantry of Solitude
>hidden in the refuge of the monk's heart

May I protect and sustain the Holy Presence
>in all relations, on our radiant Earth.

O, Benevolence, even in the shadow of error
>or pain, you shower me with riches!

O, Ocean of Mercy, the source of every comfort,
>your unwavering stillness soothes my being.

O, Mother of Compassion, you grace my soul
>with tender kisses.

May my devotion to your Pure Heart
heal our struggling world.

Amen.

MORNING PRAYER SEVEN

Canticle of Wonder

    May the dawning Light of Mystery
        enter in my cells,
        enliven my body
        and heal my wounds.

    May eternal wisdom teach me compassion
        and help the tender souls of our world.

    May all the wonders of nature
        sparrow,
        deer, meadow,
        oak and pine,
        greening hills
        and rushing streams
            join my prayer

    I draw these Earth energies into my heart.

    I breathe in and out with the breath
        of the Universal.

I breathe in deeply, divine *prana* filling
    my entire being.

I breathe out deeply, releasing all stress,
    confusion, and thought.

I open my heart to the glory of life
    and the beauty of creation,
    with joy and humility,
    in celebration of this day!

Namaste.

NOON PRAYER SEVEN

Canticle of Intimacy

Holy Wisdom:

May my heart be opened to benevolence
    my mind be stilled by beauty
    my body be filled with spirit
    my whole being a vessel for mercy

Dear Holy Wisdom
Teach me gentleness
Teach me surrender
Teach me gratitude
Teach me humility

Dear Holy Wisdom
Grant me courage
Grant me strength
Grant me fortitude
Grant me insight

May the radiant circle of
 Your Intimacy find shelter in me.

OM.

EVENING PRAYER SEVEN

Canticle of Great Silence

In the flowering meadow
Anointed by the morning dew
Shyly as petals turn toward sun
You beckon.

Shall I follow
Great Silence
Shall I abandon the noise and the need
For the longing within

You know me
I rejoice in solitude
I am sustained by emptiness
Nothing else holds

Why am I not content
With the marking of time
Why do I resist the
Kiss of possession

You beckon
And I cannot say no
You betrothed me
Great Silence
Now, I am never alone.

Amen.

Prayers *for* Days *of* Rest
and Other Occasions

Prayer to Holy Mystery

Most Holy and Unnameable Presence:

Please fill me with the fragrance of divine love
and guide me on the turbulent seas of
　　self-surrender.

Instruct me in the ways of truth,
and anoint my spirit with the beauty
　　of your holy light.

Please grant me the strength to understand
　　the nothingness,
the compassion to confront my sins,
and the patience to await the coming of
　　your word.

I enter a tabernacle of communion to draw
　　closer to you,
the one reality and splendor of my heart,
in humbleness and grace,
as I pray for the world's deliverance
from suffering and pain.

In simplicity and wonder, I open myself
to your emerging revelation
and offer myself as a birthplace
    for your new grace.

Amen.

Prayer to Holy Sophia

O Mother of Compassion
    Blessed is your heart of pure love,
        source of all life.

O Mother of Passion
    Graced are we, inflamed by the fire
        of your own desire.

O Mother of Wisdom
    Radiant is your secret teaching,
        known by the pure of heart.

O Mother of Sorrows
    You share in every wound,
        healing every suffering and sin.

O Mother of Light
    Who illuminates all realms
        with inexhaustible sweetness.

Formless, Dark Mercy
    Hidden is your power
        of wordless bliss
You are the fountain of joy
    and the breath of benevolence.

Holy Sophia, Godhead of Intimacy
    Within creation You dwell,
        longing for You alone.
Amen.

Gathering Prayer

[this prayer usually begins with the lighting of a candle]

> As we join together this day in the light of
> > Your Presence,
> we are reminded that we are all one in the
> > Divine Heart.
>
> May our longing for oneness transform
> > our world.
>
> May our hearts be opened, in the very depths
> > where we find you, God,
> to the glorious expression of your love found
> > in all religions and spiritual traditions.
>
> You speak to us, Holy Mystery, in this diversity,
> > and we are enriched and humbled by the
> breadth and depth of your Silence
> > and of your Words.

May our gathering together this day signify
> our hopes

for the harmony of our planet,
the alleviation of suffering,
food for the hungry,
shelter for the homeless,
and respect for the poor.

May this flame be a testimony of our willingness
to commit our lives to the advent of peace,
loving all and embracing all in the family
> of creation.

Amen.

Ode to Creation

In the dappled dawn
when creation breathes a still note
we find you, Majesty

We are your witness
We are your voice in the wilderness
Our feet tread lightly your mother ground

You made us like unto you
bodhicitta, holy spirit, atman, ruah
We are your body born in matter
gazing upon your own creation in us

Amen.

May We Be Worthy

May the Divine anoint our souls with the perfume
    of devotion
May the fragrant heart of divinity hold us in
    tender embrace
May the garlands of consecration adorn
    our crown,
As our shy and gentle souls bow in worship.

Blessed One, come to our aid.
May our longing be your longing
May our desire to love be fulfilled
May our hearts overflow with gratitude
In all things, may we be worthy of your gifts.

Amen.

Awaken Us

    we throw ourselves upon Mercy
    in the fiery openness of Divine Heart
        giving up our limitations,
        our possessions, our inadequacies

    remind us of the vast multitude of creation that
        groans beneath the thinnest veil of pleasure
    remind us of the hungry cries of those abandoned
        by the cruelty of our world

    attune us to the voices of the oppressed
        the silent masses of
            humanity
        our earthly kin
            rocks
            trees
            oceans
            dolphins
            owls

    awaken us, O Holy One, to the wellspring of Love.

    Amen.

Bridal Chamber of Love

May we be drawn, Gracious Spirit
to the bridal chamber of love.
Let us, in love, share your Love
with each other.

May our hearts be free of
selfishness and possession,
May we set up in the middle of history
a marriage bed, splendid and untouchable.

Amen.

Ours Hearts Become One

    We are created to love and to celebrate
        Divine Mystery in itself and in
        the bounty of creation.
    We are created within the Divine Heart
        and everything of the spirit we desire
        the Divine desires in us.
    Our being is within Divine Being.
        Our home is in the house of holiness.
    All that we are given and all that we receive
        are gifts from Divine Mystery.

    There is nothing that exits that is not spirit.

    We are given the capacity to know and love God
        directly.
    We discover the Divine in the bounty of the Earth
        and through the multiplicity of matter.
    Our journey on earth is to draw closer to the
        Divine Mystery so that our hearts become
        one Heart.

Then we are of service in the world.
    Then we are able to ignite the divine spark
    in the soul of creation.
Compassion and Love, Holy One,
    may we be your blessing.

Help Me to Remember

As I prepare myself to grow deeper in love,
May all my choices and all my desires
    be one with you, Divine Mystery.
As I move through my day,
Please help me to put aside *my* wants
    and to accept *your* intentions for me.
Please help me to remember your Presence
    in all I do.

Meditation on Silence

 1. silence
 create a space in me
  empty
   full
    for you alone

 silence
 become my breath
  deep
   strong
    for you alone

 silence
 take my heart
  rejoice
   abandon
    for you alone

 silence
 consume my soul
  nothing
   nothing
    for you alone

 2. solitude
 seize my soul
  guard my soul
   anoint my soul
 i am yours

    solitude
    companion in dark
        companion in light
            mystery incarnated
    i am yours

    solitude
    no other holds me
        no other knows me
            empty of form
    i am yours

    solitude
    my teacher
        strengthen my resolve
            command my heart
    you alone

3. emptiness
    take my identity
        leave no trace
            make me no-thing
    come!

    emptiness
    dispel my illusion
        capture my fear
            imprison my greed
    come!

emptiness
quiet my mind
    still my heart
        release my fear
come!

emptiness
lead me to freedom
    to the beginning
        to holiness itself
i am!

4. radiance

reveal my wounds
    heal my suffering
        anoint my soul
let me be light!

radiance
tender mercy
    wisdom embodied
        compassion lived
let me be light!

radiance
gentle touch
    fiery word
        ecstatic wound
let me be light!

radiance
fill me with compassion
    my wounds are nothing
        god's wound is healed
light am i!

5\. gratitude
    take me as an offering
        take my words
            take my heart
what else can i do?

gratitude
i give my name
    i give my life
        i give my gift
what else can i do?

gratitude
nothing you ask
    let me give all
        let me be all
what else can i do?

gratitude
splendor adorned!
    i bow down before you
        i kneel on hallowed ground
i am yours!

Gathering Blessing

Divine Mystery, thank you
for guiding us through the night passage,
for the gift of gathering,
for the gift of listening,
for the gift of receiving,
for the gift of insight that we share.

Sometimes we do not know where we are going
or even sure we are following the path
but we know that you love us,
that your saints surround us,
that you hold us in your merciful heart,
that there is complete transformation.

Teach us to practice nonharm.
Teach us to celebrate the beauty of life.

May we go in peace.
Amen.

Closing Benediction

> May the light of the divine shine upon us
> May the love of the divine heal
>   our struggling world,
> May the birth of the divine
>   take place
>   again and again
>   in each of our hearts.
> Amen.

Forty Days *of* Prayers

DAY 1

May I grow closer to you with each day, my dearest God. May you fill my spiritual hunger with your overflowing love.

DAY 2

Free me, Holy One, from seeking my own gratification, and conform my whole being to your loving embrace.

DAY 3

May you lead me, Great Spirit, beyond all definitions and restrictions into your heart of hearts, where the light of divine love is All.

DAY 4

I long to be alone with you, my Beloved. Please teach me the wisdom of Solitude.

DAY 5

May I be given the wisdom to be centered in my heart, O God, until my whole life is the measure of your love.

DAY 6

O, Mystery, you love me with your whole being. Please heal my wounded heart and allow me to feel the depth of your desire.

DAY 7

May I feel, Divine One, the passion of your love for those who suffer and are downtrodden by the sins of the world.

DAY 8

Humble me, my God, until my heart overflows with gratitude for all the blessings you bestow on me this day.

DAY 9

O, Divine Mother, may my heart be opened to the suffering of women and girls, and may our communities heal the violence against our beloved sisters everywhere.

DAY 10

Silent Wonder, your creation is full of splendor and mystery! May your compassion heal my spiritual wounds and help me honor the beauty of my difference.

DAY 11

Show me, Holy One, how I may draw closer to you in daily life. Give me the courage to seek you alone in all I do and all I am.

DAY 12

May I have the determination and the faith to journey with You, in both the trials and joys of every day.

DAY 13

O Beloved, make me strong so I may give away my small self, and make me weak so I may become simple and pure of heart.

DAY 14

In every struggle, dear God, you have bound me to your heart. Help me to learn from my trials, suffering the power of love.

DAY 15

Ignite my soul, Divine Mother, with the Holy Spirit's fire, and set me free from bondage. May your freedom become the emblem of my devotion.

DAY 16

May your dark light of wisdom penetrate my soul and help me to seek you more each day. It is for you, Holy One, that my parched soul thirsts.

DAY 17

Teach me, O Peace, how to be quiet and strong in myself. Grant me the serenity of wisdom, so that I may remember that You alone sustain the fluttering of my heart.

DAY 18

As I weep with tears of fire, may the love of the Divine soothe my weary soul.

DAY 19

O God of justice and peace! Please open my heart and the hearts of all humanity to the suffering of women and men, and the subjugation of the feminine spirit of life.

DAY 20

Help me, Loving Creator, to accept your gifts with a humble heart. May I honor my limitations and the limitations of others as I grow in peace and serenity.

DAY 21

May your light shine on me, Holy One, until my soul is made humble and free. Take me and use me for your work of reconciliation in the world.

DAY 22

Console me, Divine Mother, as the storms of change tear down my limitations and build up my longing for your life. Grant me the courage of faith.

DAY 23

Dear God, I know you are with me in my strength and in my weakness. Show me how to celebrate weakness as a sign of peace and truth.

DAY 24

May my heart overflow with compassion for the suffering of humanity everywhere. May you help me, Loving Creator, to practice nonviolence of spirit.

DAY 25

Divine Mother of us all, help my heart and the heart of our world to clamor for peace. In the name of suffering humanity everywhere, lament with us and show us the way to relief and healing.

DAY 26

Come to life in me, each day, Holy One. Help me to turn all my worries over to You who fills the universe with joy.

DAY 27

Gentle Spirit, marry silence and speech, prayer and action in my own heart. Teach me the wisdom of being united, one in one, in the cosmic unfolding of your magnificence.

DAY 28

Silence, Great Teacher, fill my soul with your perfume! May you find shelter in my heart and lead me to feel the pulsing of creation toward holiness.

DAY 29

O, Joyous One! How I long to laugh with you; how I long to wash away all my tears! Your boundless happiness adorns my heart with song.

DAY 30

May my heart expand without words into the silence of your love. Anoint me, Divine One, with the wisdom of the unseen.

DAY 31

Today, and all the days of my life, grant me the strength to examine my heart. May I be faithful, God, to your gift of truth in me.

DAY 32

May my heart groan with those who are pained and feel anguish with those who suffer oppression. May my soul feel your sorrow and concern, Darling Mother, for our world.

DAY 33

Blessed are you, Creator, for the many souls of light that have illuminated my path. May their memory and the memory of all your saints shine with compassion on our Earth.

DAY 34

As you have bestowed mercy on us, O God, may my heart grow in love and forgiveness for my own and others' sins. Lead me to your inner sanctum, to the white light of union.

DAY 35

Show me, Fount of Mercy, where I can find you! Come to me, Merciful One, and be a rudder for my wandering soul.

DAY 36

Thank you for all the friends in my life. Thank you for their love and honesty. May I become a more committed and generous person in all my relations.

DAY 37

Thank you for the freedom to question. Thank you for the joy of not knowing. My heart is humble before your glory.

DAY 38

Blessed be you, who bestows all Goodness. Blessed be you, heart of hearts. Blessed be you, who contemplates life through creation.

DAY 39

Each day, I practice the three wisdoms—love, humility, and emptiness. I long to learn to be my best on the other side of pain and loss.

DAY 40

O, glorious Light, how my soul is illumined by your radiance! In all of creation you are hidden by the most tender of veils.

Prayer *of the*
Universal Monk

Why I am a Universal Monk
(To be read singly or in community)

In light of the intense suffering of our planet
   in the illumination of the mystical oneness of life
I need to express the depth of my feeling for Divine Mystery
   suffusing my soul with longing and devotion.
I offer myself to God in a gesture of complete gift
   in response to the unconditional gift I have been given.
I wish to reveal the intensity of my passion for the
   mysterious energy that loves me without motive or design.
I vow to uphold the dignity of all beings
   to prepare myself to be an oasis of compassion.
I affirm the solitary basis of existence and communion with
   the Alone, who gives meaning to my every breath.

The monastic vocation draws me into the cave of the heart
   centering me in *The Center*,
     detaching me from the noise and digressions of the world.
The monastic heart is a lover of the cosmos
   and yearns to be in service of the Holy.
Pulled into the chamber of solitude, I am married to silence
   and taught in secret of a reality with no name.

Here I find my greatest happiness as my whole being
  is inflamed by love of the sacred.
From my earliest youth I have been a monk without a habit,
  a contemplative without a home, living between realms.
Transfigured by an understanding of a new spiritual life,
  my soul suffers the divisions that wound the radiant Oneness.
If my heart were not open to the gift of divine benevolence,
  my vows would be naught.

I am a universal monk, an interspiritual, global monk,
  embracing the fullness of humanity's spiritual quest,
  even as I live my own unique version.
For in the monastic heart that precedes every religious name,
  the contemplative vow is uttered.
This state of consciousness touches the original blueprint,
  the wombing place of archetypes and forms.

I am a universal monk because I was called in the beginning
  to experience suffering over our separation and exclusion.
Commanded by Love to embrace every religion and
  spirituality, I am not allowed to privilege one over another.

I am a universal monk because I strive to live each day
   by the vows and commandments given to me,
   offering to others the freedom and hope that I myself
   am granted.

I am a universal monk, a global monk, because my
   monkhood extends beyond myself to embrace
   all the inhabitants of Earth and cosmos.

I am a universal monk because I have offered my soul
   as a site of unity and a home for the homeless
   in silence, in solitude flourishing with love of the world
   for its own sake
   for love alone.

I am a universal monk who would be bereft
   without the steady force that guides me
   without the community that shares my heart's desire
   for a planet of peace and happiness.

I am a monk who stands in protest to the agreement
   we humans make
   and the violence we humans inflict on the holy.

I commit myself and my soul
> to the transformation of our hearts
> to an ideal more noble and more compassionate.

I am a monk because I was called and I answered,
> Yes.

Books by Beverly Lanzetta

A New Silence:
Spiritual Practices and Formation for the Monk Within
ISBN 978-1-7323438-3-2

The Monk Within:
Embracing a Sacred Way of Life
ISBN 978-0-9840616-5-5

Foundations in Spiritual Direction:
Sharing the Sacred Across Traditions
ISBN 978-0-9840616-0-0

Path of the Heart:
A Spiritual Guide to Divine Union
ISBN 978-0-9840616-2-4

Nine Jewels of Night:
One Soul's Journey into God
ISBN 978-0-9840616-1-7

Emerging Heart:
Global Spirituality and the Sacred
ISBN 978-0-8006-3893-1

40 Day Journey with Joan Chittister
ISBN 978-0-8066-8031-6

Radical Wisdom:
A Feminist Mystical Theology
ISBN 0-8006-3698-8

The Other Side of Nothingness:
Toward a Theology of Radical Openness
ISBN 0-7914-4950-5

BEVERLY LANZETTA, Ph.D. is a theologian, spiritual teacher, and the author of many groundbreaking books on emerging global spirituality and new monasticism, including *The Monk Within: Embracing a Sacred Way of Life*, *Radical Wisdom: A Feminist Mystical Theology*, *Emerging Heart: Global Spirituality and the Sacred*, and *Nine Jewels of Night: One Soul's Journey into God*. A monk of peace, she is dedicated to a vision of theological openness and spiritual nonviolence; her work has won praise for its wisdom, eloquence, and mystical insight and is considered to be a major contribution to what theologian Ursula King called "a feminine mystical way for the 21st century." Dr. Lanzetta has taught theology at Villanova University, Prescott College, and Grinnell College and has started a number of religious and monastic initiatives including the Desert Interfaith Church, Interfaith Theological Seminary, Hesychia School of Spiritual Direction, and the Community of a New Monastic Way. She is a much-sought-after mentor for the new generation, including the "spiritual but not religious" and new monastics alike, as she brings with her forty years of experience as a guide to answering the universal call to contemplation.

www.ingramcontent.com/pod-product-compliance
Lightning Source LLC
Chambersburg PA
CBHW051955290426
44110CB00015B/2248